Lena Ma
The Passion Of My Desolation

Lena Ma
The Passion Of My Desolation

Lena Ma
The Passion Of My Desolation

The Passion Of My Desolation

Lena Ma
The Passion Of My Desolation

Lena Ma
The Passion Of My Desolation

The Passion Of My Desolation

By Lena Ma

© Copyright 2021

Lena Ma
The Passion Of My Desolation

Lena Ma
The Passion Of My Desolation

Table of Contents

The Blade Of My Right Hand
12

My Heart, I Surrender
18

Terminal Faith
23

My Last Journey, Forever
28

Without You, I Feel Nothing
33

Lena Ma
The Passion Of My Desolation

The Comfort Of My Piercing Needle
38

Blood Seeps In My Silent Battle
43

A World Where I Don't Belong
48

The Queen Behind The Screen
52

A Robotic Slave
57

Chasing Wind
61

Lena Ma
The Passion Of My Desolation

Seize The Darkness, End The Light
66

Survival Of Endless Nights
70

Disappearance At Conception
74

Lady Misfortune
78

Nothing But Scars Left Behind
82

Stabbing Shadows From My Past
86

Lena Ma
The Passion Of My Desolation

Individuality Behind The Mask
91

Tragedy That Is My Existence
95

Trapped Inside My Treacherous Body
99

Lust In My Champagne
103

Lena Ma
The Passion Of My Desolation

Lena Ma
The Passion Of My Desolation

The Blade Of My Right Hand

Lena Ma
The Passion Of My Desolation

The pain I feel deep inside is like none I have ever experienced before.
The expression of my woes leaves me speechless and cold.
My heart is dead; my blood runs still; my soul always yearning for more,
Even as the days pass me, my eyes cry for you as I turn old.

They say time heals all wounds, and your betrayal will soon be forgotten,
What they don't realize is how swiftly you came into my life, like a sweet, summer breeze,
Allowing me to trust you, love you, believe in you, now leaving my memories rotten.
I opened myself to you, vulnerable, and you brought me to my knees.

Lena Ma
The Passion Of My Desolation

I thought you were different; I thought you were real.
You pushed me to the ground, left me in tears for what you have done.
I thought you were perfect, the way you made me feel,
And I knew I had to leave, but you took away my courage to run.

You stabbed me with a knife and betrayed me when I was down.
I lie awake at night, haunted by our endless fights,
Memories of you suffocating me as I feel ready to drown.
With you gone, I can finally enter the light.

Lena Ma
The Passion Of My Desolation

We were so close, so connected, never knowing what we may find.
I knew they changed you, tampering your brain, turning you corrupt.
The others who came and went wounded my body, but you wounded my mind.
Times are different now; I'm ready to give up.

I can still hear your voice; the stillness inside me will never fade away.
You tell me we will never be the same as you watch me burn up in flames.
I cry for help; I cry for you, knowing you will never stay.
I blame myself, while you stand there holding onto my shame.

Lena Ma
The Passion Of My Desolation

I miss you, my friend, goodbye forever as I feel myself nearing death.
With this blade I forgive you, as I take my final breath.

Lena Ma
The Passion Of My Desolation

Lena Ma
The Passion Of My Desolation

My Heart, I Surrender

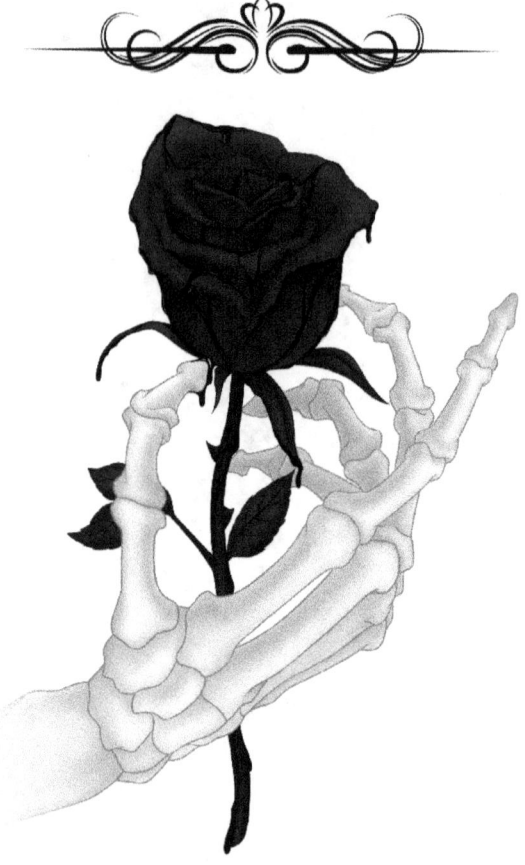

Lena Ma
The Passion Of My Desolation

My friend, my lover, I have only myself to blame.
On you, I placed my life, your trust I can never amend.
You hear me call for you, my hand reaching out, screaming your name,
But you ignore me, turning away, like it was all pretend.

I can clearly remember the day we met,
Your hair golden brown, and your eyes ocean blue.
I never met someone so different, placing my life in you like a gambler's bet.
I was so naïve; I loved you, but I didn't have a clue.

Lena Ma
The Passion Of My Desolation

But now times are changing, life moving on like you never cared.
You were always by my side, wiping the sadness away from my eyes.
The infidelity, the lies, the deceit, leaving me alone and scared,
Tightly holding onto the little we had as our knot unties.

As I drown inside this bottle, I drink away my sorrows.
I've watched many come and go; I thought, indeed, you were the one.
It doesn't matter anymore, for I know there's no tomorrow.
There's no turning back now as I am finally done.

Lena Ma
The Passion Of My Desolation

What happened to us? I will always wonder.
Your wish I grant you; you are now released.
I hear the thunder now, pouring down as I finally surrender,
I hope you live your life; I hope you find peace.

Lena Ma
The Passion Of My Desolation

Lena Ma
The Passion Of My Desolation

Terminal Faith

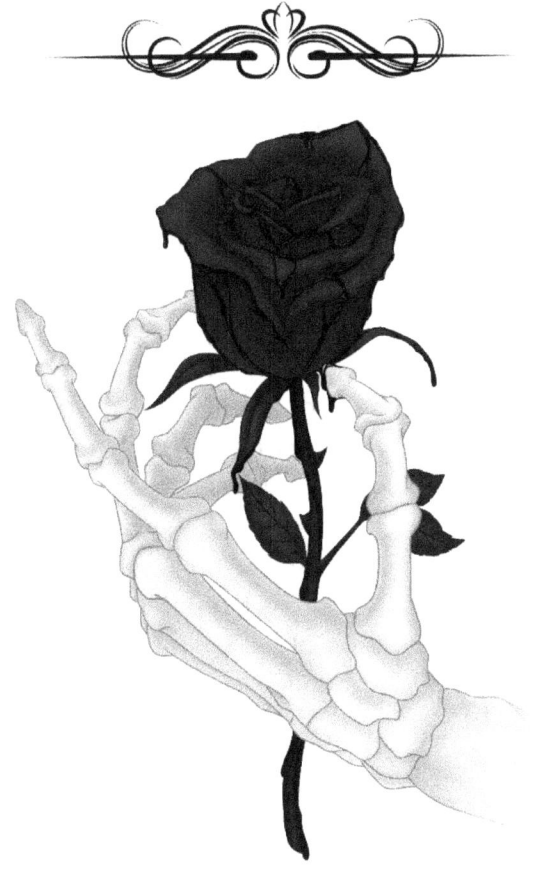

Lena Ma
The Passion Of My Desolation

My faith is lost; I cannot hide.
My heart locked in a cage, my mind splashing with rage; I wish I could heal.
My time is near, no time for fear; I know I've tried.
My life feels different now, everything so surreal.

Trying to withhold my fears, I wonder how I got here,
Screaming into my mirror, no longer recognizing the face staring back.
It's consuming my body; each day, a part of me disappears.
My life used to be perfect, but now all I see is black.

Lena Ma
The Passion Of My Desolation

This illness changed me into someone I never thought I'd be,
Though I can't complain too much, as I know others are equally in pain.
Locked up in my caged thoughts, despising the days I used to be free.
I can't continue this fight; my blood continues to drain.

I used to be so carefree, now, questioning the meaning of life.
Regretting the moments I took for granted, choices and decisions I had made.
Many mistakes, numerous enemies, all ending in strife,
Moments I've spent in pride and hatred when I should have been afraid.

Lena Ma
The Passion Of My Desolation

My time is ending, my family crying as I lie here no longer with faith.
My heart cold as ice, with endless pain that no one can measure.
I'm dying, I tell myself, my mind spinning with wraith,
Leaving the world I lived in, the one that gave me so much pleasure.

Lena Ma
The Passion Of My Desolation

Lena Ma
The Passion Of My Desolation

My Last Journey, Forever

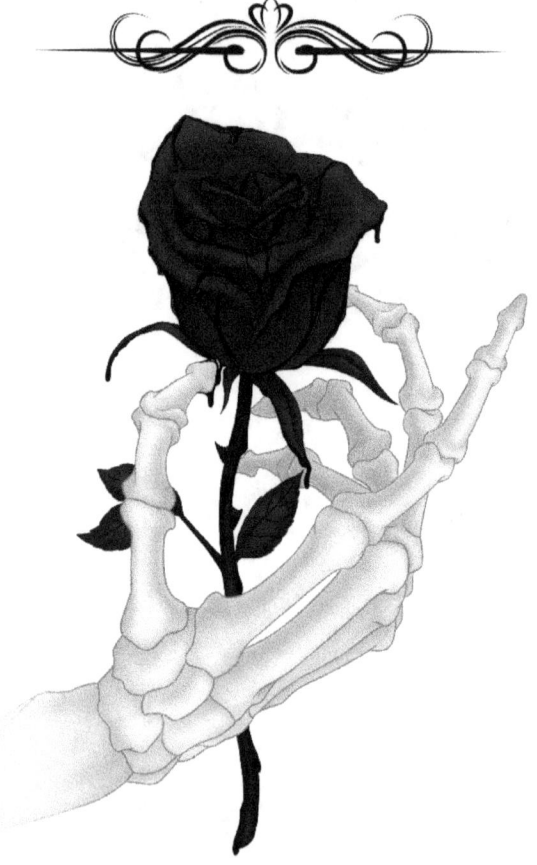

Lena Ma
The Passion Of My Desolation

I look over at my desk, bare as the day I first walked in,
My youth decaying in this box as I face the cold, hard truth.
Believing I would die here was nothing more than a sin.
Only one thing can numb me, a glass of vermouth.

I was so innocent, so excited, the day I was hired,
Devoting my entire life, watching all the rest slowly slip away,
Never really expecting the day I might be fired.
The struggles were real, now regretting all the years I decided to stay.

Lena Ma
The Passion Of My Desolation

I watched others come and go as I continued to climb the peak,
Secretly lavishing in all the moments when others slipped.
I thought I was special; I thought I was unique,
Karma hitting hard when I finally lost my grip.

The sun continues to descend, my life now turning grey,
If only it wasn't too late to take back all that I have lost.
We don't admit it, but everyone eventually falls to prey.
No longer can I turn back, revisit all the roads I have crossed.

Lena Ma
The Passion Of My Desolation

My heart yearns for adventure, but my body has become too frail.
My quest for happiness now much too rare, my shadows suffering in despair.
Walking through the darkness, knowing I can never prevail,
Removing myself from those I've disappointed; my life in solitaire.

I stumble across the tracks, the train heading towards me as I wave my last goodbye.
I hop on, ready to leave this life behind as fate takes my body away.
My life has been nothing but a waste, that I cannot deny.
Whatever happens, I am ready to decay.

Lena Ma
The Passion Of My Desolation

Lena Ma
The Passion Of My Desolation

Without You, I Feel Nothing

Lena Ma
The Passion Of My Desolation

Sleepless nights, I face, the day you became ill,
The pain of losing you forever keeps me sad and awake.
Depressed, I become, every night I see you still,
The memory of your touch, your embrace, I feel my heart ache.

I wish I could hug you, kiss you, heal all your pain.
I would do anything, everything, just to hear your voice.
I wish I could stop the horror coursing through your veins,
If only times were different, if only you had a choice.

Lena Ma
The Passion Of My Desolation

Memories of my childhood, I hold onto so dear.
I can still feel the skin of your hand against the skin of mine.
Mother, I miss you, I wish you were here.
You will forever be my Savior, my angel, my divine.

Every night I look for you among the falling stars.
I can no longer face society without fighting back my tears.
I try so hard, but nothing can hide away my scars.
I can never bring you back, but you'll always be in my prayers.

Lena Ma
The Passion Of My Desolation

You told me to never suffer, and now I feel ashamed.
Whatever happened to the days when I was simply just afraid?
It's time for me to go, just like I came, unnamed.
I took you for granted, my best friend, I betrayed.

Lena Ma
The Passion Of My Desolation

Lena Ma
The Passion Of My Desolation

The Comfort Of My Piercing Needle

Lena Ma
The Passion Of My Desolation

You made me trust you, believe you were my remedy.
You loved me dearly as I let you embrace my veins.
I thought I would be cool, develop a better identity,
Instead, you destroyed me, your breath worse than cocaine.

I need to get out, leave, scared of what I'll say,
When I lie to those I love, blind to who I see in my mirror.
But every time I run, you always convince me to stay,
For without you with me, I become angry and bitter.

Lena Ma
The Passion Of My Desolation

Who have I become? What have I turned into?
It hurts so much, the scars no one can see.
How did I become so dependent, helpless,
hopeless, without you?
I feel so lost, so broken, someone please help
me.

You made me your slave, ravished my body
and drove me insane.
Every night I slumber alone, you haunt my
sleep and come knocking.
Too late for regrets and sorrow, the days I shall
never regain.
Nothing surprises me anymore, nothing I find
shocking.

Lena Ma
The Passion Of My Desolation

My hands cold, my heart blackens, I've become sick of relapsing.
Even as I gasp, no one will aid my pleading cries.
My eyes burn deep; why does this keep happening?
No one to my rescue, all stuck between my truth and lies.

I'm all alone now, waiting for my end.
I used to have it all, trophies and certificates on my shelf.
This piercing needle and glass, now my only friends.
Who am I? I no longer know. End my life as I kill myself.

Lena Ma
The Passion Of My Desolation

Lena Ma
The Passion Of My Desolation

Blood Seeps In My Silent Battle

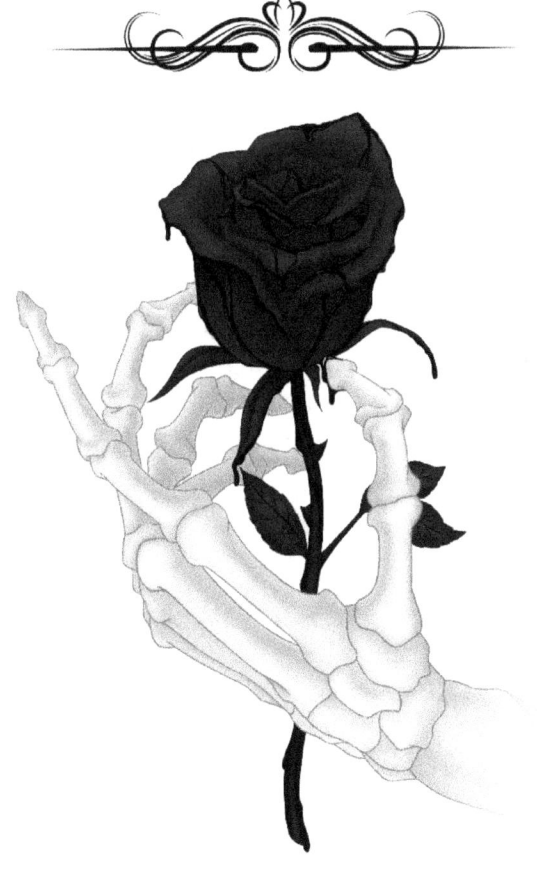

Lena Ma
The Passion Of My Desolation

Am I good enough yet for the perfection that you desire?
Starving myself days on end so one day I'll be worthy.
I know I've gone too far, the consequences soon be dire,
But self-hate and pain come second to feeling pretty.

This vicious cycle plagues my mind, sharp misery and blind.
The angry demon chasing me as I reach for perfection.
Never letting go, even as my health declines.
I can no longer look at myself, repulsed at my reflection.

Lena Ma
The Passion Of My Desolation

Another pound is much more than I can ever bear.
I push others away so I can let no one else down.
My claws digging into my skin, every regret forming a tear,
I refuse to cease my silent battle until I fit into my gown.

I can feel the sickness in my blood, struggling to escape.
They lock me up, everyone gone, I pushed them all away.
Cracked lips and tired eyes forming so I can stay in shape,
Lying in this cell alone, my mind my body obeys.

Lena Ma
The Passion Of My Desolation

Just be strong, I tell myself, as I lift the fork to my mouth.
Fear and anxiety seep down my hand, tears flowing from my eyes.
"Don't do it," it whispers, a voice I cannot live without.
I place it back down, for tomorrow, I will not rise.

Lena Ma
The Passion Of My Desolation

Lena Ma
The Passion Of My Desolation

A World Where I Don't Belong

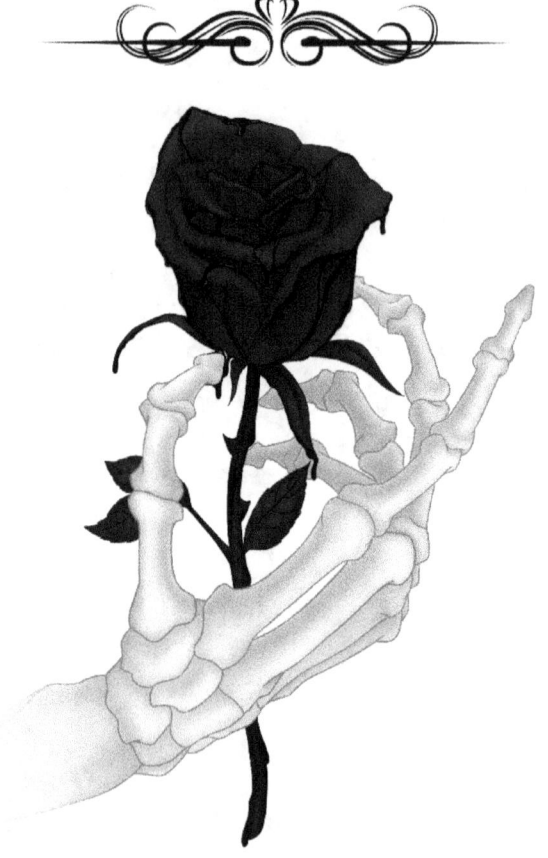

Lena Ma
The Passion Of My Desolation

A child born humble into an ever-changing world,
Yet all I see are people, apartheid still grasped strong across their minds.
My ethnicity and skin still course on every page curled,
I thought times had changed, everyone matured, but maybe we're all just blind.

You call it harmless, but my heart throbs with each passing comment.
Exposing me as a flaw, a degenerate, a life deserved to end.
Split between my own image and yours as I'm overwhelmed with lament,
We're all the same, yet on you, my life depends.

Lena Ma
The Passion Of My Desolation

Human crudeness at its finest; ignorance surely is bliss.
Judge me by my skin, accusing me without a brain.
Intolerance is acceptable, only on your terms we cannot dismiss.
We're all equally insecure; that's why we place the blame.

We have come too far to live life in this segregation.
Fighting too hard to live in a world free from contention.
We never change, from generation to generation,
Isolating others and tearing them down, all just for attention.

Lena Ma
The Passion Of My Desolation

Lena Ma
The Passion Of My Desolation

The Queen Behind The Screen

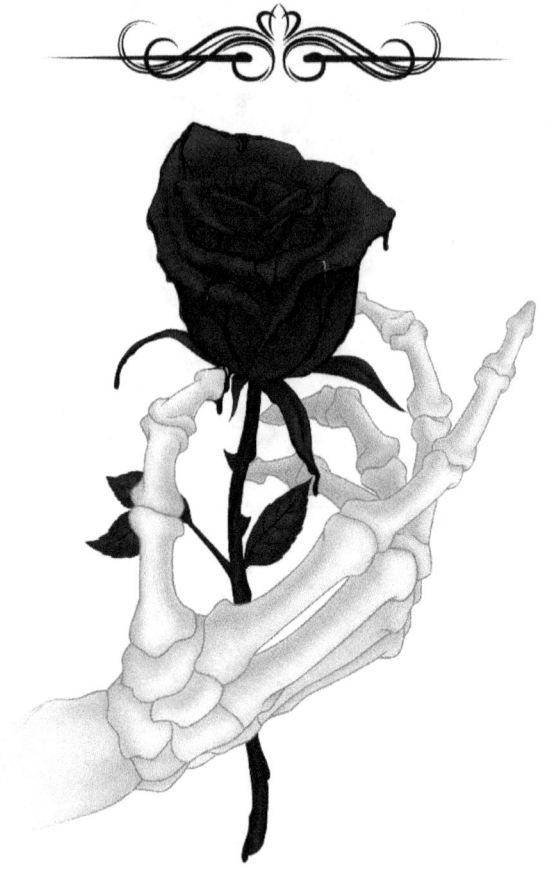

Lena Ma
The Passion Of My Desolation

I hate you, but I can never say it to your face.
Rather, leaving open wounds on a page for others to stab.
I find joy in this heartless game I'm trying to chase,
Picking and picking until I'm no longer a scab.

I know you're hurting, crying on the other side.
But I can't stop, finding strength in the numbness I possess.
You've approached me, confronted me, but I've denied,
That I, your best friend, ruining your life, I obsess.

Lena Ma
The Passion Of My Desolation

I find peace in my offensive words, gaining attention with each hateful post.
Others say I'm inspiring, living out my best dreams.
You think I'm conniving, but it's really me who I hate the most.
My smile hidden deeper inside, far beneath my screams.

I hear the words I call you, "ugly", "fat", but at least you know who you really are.
Your resilience as you endure each hateful word makes you that much stronger.
I judge because I know I can never be, never go far,
That's why I sit alone, in the dark, a true, miserable loner.

Lena Ma
The Passion Of My Desolation

You try to manage your pain and agony, but at least yours are genuine.
You cry, and you hate, but at least you're aware it's all fake,
While I establish my place hidden on the Internet like a true denizen,
Living a lie behind a screen, unaware if I'm asleep or awake.

Lena Ma
The Passion Of My Desolation

Lena Ma
The Passion Of My Desolation

A Robotic Slave

Lena Ma
The Passion Of My Desolation

"Stay humble, grow up rich," they always said to me.
Chase the dream of nine to five; you'll never have to worry.
For several decades, I listened, unable to breathe.
I should never have obeyed; here is my story.

This delusion I'm stuck in, with constant worries of whether I'll make it.
I'm drowning in the hands of debt, never being released,
Trying to fight against it for crimes I did commit,
Forever trapped and surrounded, until I become deceased.

Lena Ma
The Passion Of My Desolation

I never wanted my life to end this way.
It started off so innocent, the simple things I bought.
My life crumbling down soon after I could not pay,
The hell I'm in, from a small hole, I thought.

I thought I had it all, the filthy rich holding all the land,
Before becoming a slave to the system with no way out.
If only I had stayed humble and lived life like I planned,
I wouldn't be burying my grave, just to reach for clout.

Lena Ma
The Passion Of My Desolation

Lena Ma
The Passion Of My Desolation

Chasing Wind

Lena Ma
The Passion Of My Desolation

I walk alone deep into the forest, the quiet wind blowing through the trees.
My thoughts begin to slow, my mind entering a deep sleep.
My heart beats slowly as I fall down to my knees,
My emotions running wild, my eyes beginning to weep.

My entire life I spent chasing after my dreams,
Trying so hard to be part of the shallow crowd,
Just to find out that no one is who they seem.
Now, I walk alone on a floating cloud.

Lena Ma
The Passion Of My Desolation

Why do I always chase the love that can never be?
Struggling to find my way back when I fall through the cracks,
Leaving me stranded in the deep ocean sea,
Always leaving myself vulnerable to get stabbed in the back.

I've always dreamt of someone who can take me by the hand,
But instead, I find myself completely empty inside.
The more I scream for attention, the less they understand.
I've lived my whole life as a lie so no one can see I've tried.

Lena Ma
The Passion Of My Desolation

Nothing matters anymore; all will be lost when my life soon ends.
My thoughts so overwhelming that I can't even explain.
I'm done trying, no longer will I need to pretend,
As I leave the world the same I entered, my body remains.

Lena Ma
The Passion Of My Desolation

Lena Ma
The Passion Of My Desolation

Seize The Darkness, End The Light

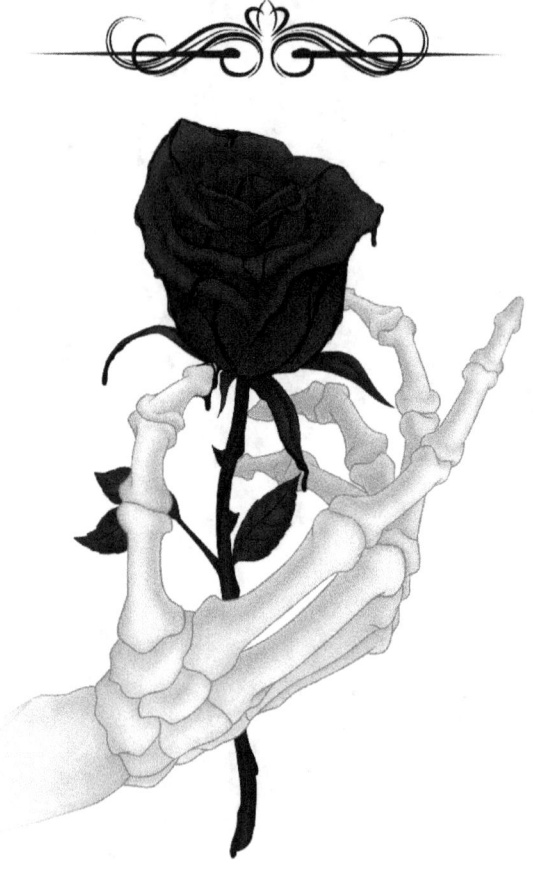

Lena Ma
The Passion Of My Desolation

My soul has been destroyed from the misery I feel,
My life becoming depressed with no meaning left behind.
I live in a world of oppression with nothing that can heal,
If only everyone wasn't so naïve, wasn't so blind.

Feelings of dismay lie deep inside my body; memories washed away.
My thoughts begin to swirl as I cry, darkness seizing the light.
The emotions are too intense, yet they tell me to seize the day,
No matter how hard I've tried, I will always lose the fight.

Lena Ma
The Passion Of My Desolation

From endless pain to dark depression, my tears fill with sorrow,
Drowning deeper and deeper with no one to my avail.
No longer do I seize onto hope, waiting for a better tomorrow,
Darkness has consumed me, minimal light remains.

My days of struggle have only left me insane,
The ridicule and torture drive away my will to fight.
I used to be proud, living solely in vain,
Now I'm wasting away, hellfire into the night.

Lena Ma
The Passion Of My Desolation

Lena Ma
The Passion Of My Desolation

Survival Of Endless Nights

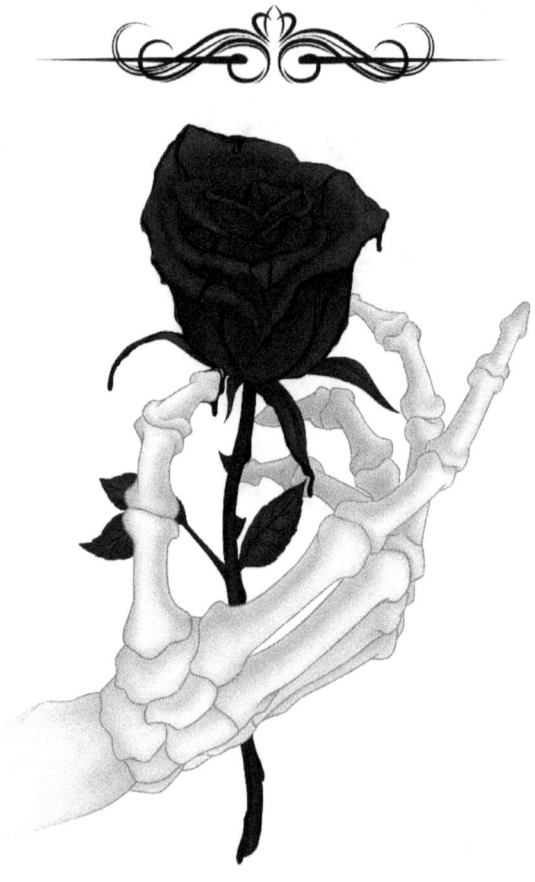

Lena Ma
The Passion Of My Desolation

Crippling paralysis, silent screams, when will this nightmare end?
Panic worries and darkness surrounds, smiles plastered on my face.
My mind so afraid, my body so numb, I can only pretend,
That I'm just like you despite praying for God's saving grace.

Not a day passes by without internal fights and endless nights.
My heart compresses, and I find myself unable to breathe.
Feeling like the world has turned against me, leaving me in fright,
Leaving me trembling and shaking on my knees.

Lena Ma
The Passion Of My Desolation

This isn't my body; someone please find me.
This feels so unreal, so alone, so unfair.
Fear is the enemy, please just set me free,
These constant battles inside me leaving me impaired.

I cannot leave my home, cannot function in society.
Even the thought of stepping out makes it hard for me to swallow.
No one can understand, inside my mind the ferocity,
I lie awake restless, night after night, hoping for a better tomorrow.

Lena Ma
The Passion Of My Desolation

Lena Ma
The Passion Of My Desolation

Disappearance At Conception

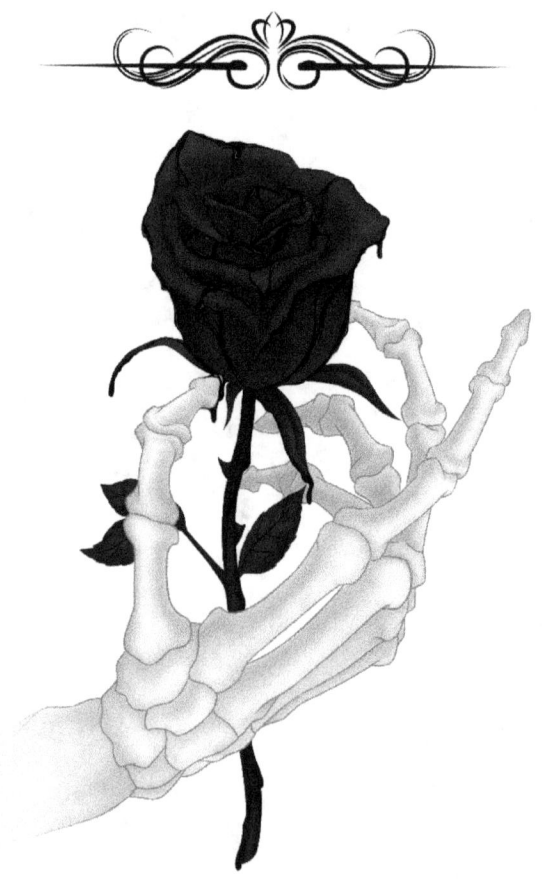

Lena Ma
The Passion Of My Desolation

A lonely child, desperate for attention,
Crying out for mom and dad, just to remain ignored.
Being around them just overwhelms me with tension,
Locked up and barred, my life unexplored.

I shall never know the damage I have done,
The horrors they blame me for, which I cannot even understand.
I wish I could take it back, the words that left me shunned,
Living in this household, forgotten and under fire, is too much to withstand.

Lena Ma
The Passion Of My Desolation

I feel so unwanted, so abandoned, so detached,
Please forgive me, don't lock me behind closed doors.
What have I done, why our bond has become unlatched?
All I ever wanted was a family, to be part of yours.

You ridicule when I cry; you mock when I seek aid,
Never noticing the insanity you have all driven me into.
You played me like a fool; I feel so betrayed,
I'm just a scared child, with absolutely no one to turn to.

Lena Ma
The Passion Of My Desolation

Lena Ma
The Passion Of My Desolation

Lady Misfortune

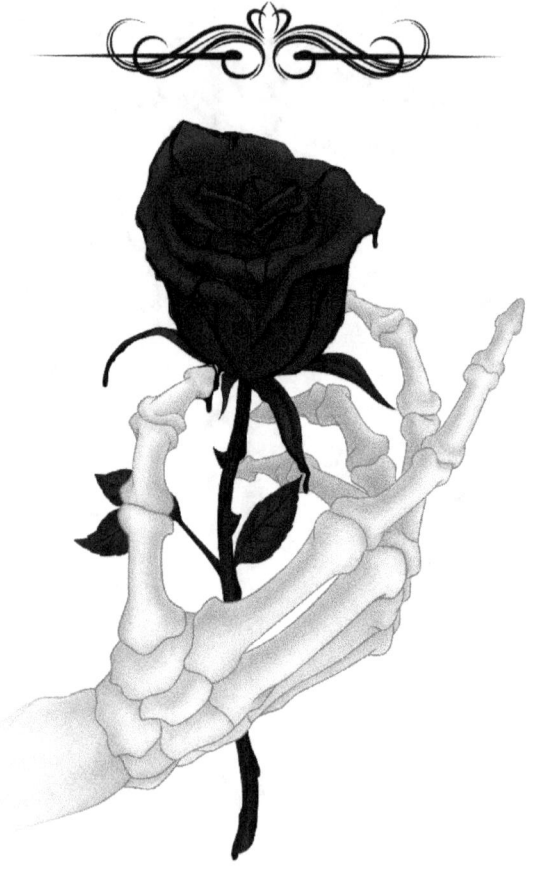

Lena Ma
The Passion Of My Desolation

I cannot get up today, my body shivering beneath the sheets,
Face buried in my pillow, sweat pouring down my face.
I'm terrified of this existence, every night it repeats,
To my species, I am nothing but a disgrace.

Is it life that I fear or maybe just my own shadow?
Is it the mistakes I have made or simply the ones I foresee?
I wish my thoughts didn't lie so deep; I wish they weren't so hollow,
I wish I could just forget; my soul please set me free.

Lena Ma
The Passion Of My Desolation

The misfortune of this world will soon come to an end,
All the tragedies in my life will set sail with the passing wind.
I've wasted my life under these sheets, hoping my mind would transcend,
Now it's all gone, ending before it can even begin.

Why do I dread the woes I cannot even comprehend?
Feeling so anxious that my world would crumble down.
The words "brave" and "courage", I will never understand,
My whole life I've been lost, never to be found.

Lena Ma
The Passion Of My Desolation

Lena Ma
The Passion Of My Desolation

Nothing But Scars Left Behind

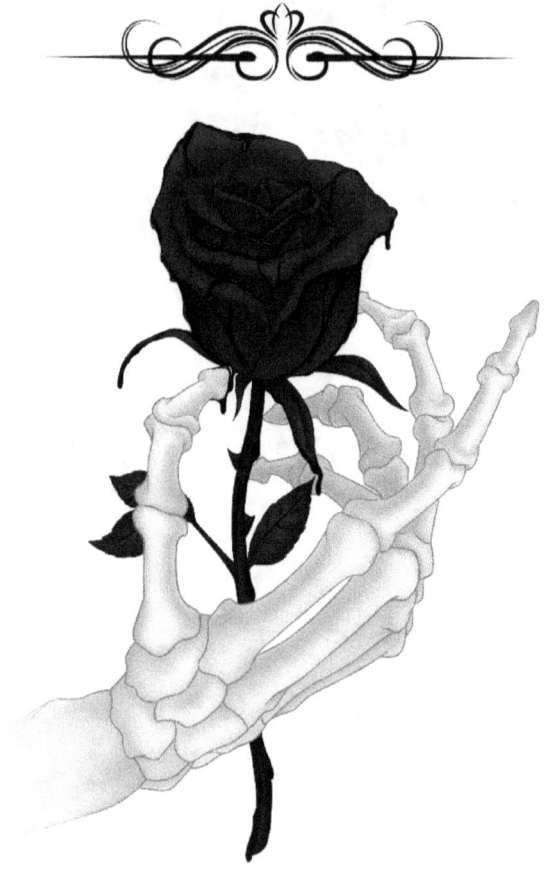

Lena Ma
The Passion Of My Desolation

I fade away as the seasons change,
Already regretting the choices I have made.
Every time I speak, I feel so deranged,
As I have accomplished nothing over this past decade.

Who am I without a legacy to leave behind?
Gambling on my own life with never a fighting chance.
They warned me to quit early, to their words I was so blind,
Now I roam the streets, living in a trance.

Lena Ma
The Passion Of My Desolation

I try to change my life, but in its way is my aggression,
Seeking answers only I want to know,
Never realizing that I am falling into deep depression,
Until the day comes where it's time for me to go.

My life has no meaning; I am nothing but a scar,
Placed on this Earth as a blemish.
I thought I could go far; I thought I could become a star,
Instead, I'm left with nothing, from the grounds I will soon perish.

Lena Ma
The Passion Of My Desolation

Lena Ma
The Passion Of My Desolation

Stabbing Shadows From My Past

Lena Ma
The Passion Of My Desolation

"Stop," I cried, to the flashbacks that still haunt me.
Just a young girl attempting to evade the shadows.
But he didn't stop, continuing to turn the key,
Pressing me down as he promised a better tomorrow.

No one would listen; no one would hear,
Holding in my tears as he continued to pursue,
As I stayed silent, my voice powerless to fear,
All of these memories I wish I could undo.

Lena Ma
The Passion Of My Desolation

I feel so exposed, so broken, my thoughts continue to haunt,
Even as the years pass, the pain continues to overwhelm.
I lie in bed at night, the sheets continuing to taunt,
Like beautiful rose petals, blown from their stems.

The frightened screams and stabbing shadows follow me for decades,
Flashes of teeth and ropes keeping me up at night.
For so long, I've wanted peace, like an end of a soft serenade,
But I feel myself fading, transitioning to a lady in white.

Lena Ma
The Passion Of My Desolation

I will never forget him, the one who stole my life,
The one who took away my innocence and left me nothing but rage.
Because of him, I can never find the hope of becoming a wife,
The glee I deserved no longer exists, trapped alone in this tiny cage.

Lena Ma
The Passion Of My Desolation

Lena Ma
The Passion Of My Desolation

Individuality Behind The Mask

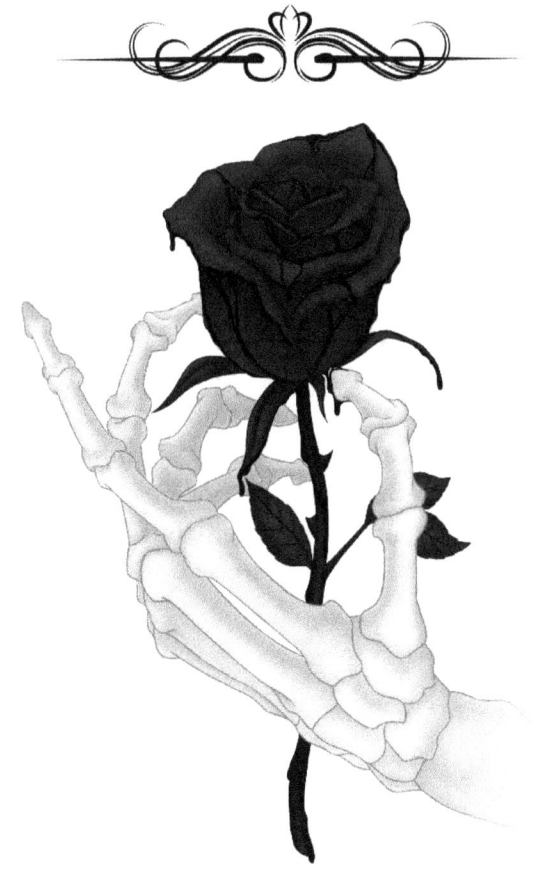

Lena Ma
The Passion Of My Desolation

To be part of society requires the relinquishing of your individuality,
Leaving us with this nightmare of darkness and confusion.
I tried so hard to belong that I gave up my personality,
Leaving me with nothing, but delusion and illusion.

Everywhere we look, we see the uprise of more and more clones,
Until the point where we no longer recognize the person in the mirror.
Similar voices, plastic masks surround, all chilling to the bone,
I hate turning into one of them, but I can see no way clearer.

Lena Ma
The Passion Of My Desolation

Conformity has now become the common norm,
Fitting into the standard mold or else live in disarray.
I used to be special, unique, before I transformed,
Now simply trapped behind a shell, my person not on display.

They roam the streets and conquer the Internet,
Unable to distinguish fantasy from reality.
True individuality and substance we all soon forget,
Stuck in this never-ending world of lust and tragedy.

Lena Ma
The Passion Of My Desolation

Lena Ma
The Passion Of My Desolation

Tragedy That Is My Existence

Lena Ma
The Passion Of My Desolation

I shall never be accomplished, my peers far more successful,
I shall never be beautiful, my flaws consuming my face.
I cannot breathe; my body remains in an empty vessel,
Of nothingness, my mind and body misplaced.

I want to be like her, confident and glamorous,
Instead, I find in myself loathing and weakness,
Hiding behind shadows so others won't find me cancerous.
Knowing I'm just different, with definitely no uniqueness.

Lena Ma
The Passion Of My Desolation

They ask me how I am, the timid girl sitting in silence.
I respond with positivity, concealing the battle inside my mind.
No one needs to know that behind this smile is pure violence,
Against myself as my mind and body decline.

I hate my existence, just consuming space reserved for others.
I need it to be over, my eyes blinded to the person I perceive.
I am not wanted; no one will ever see my true colors,
If only I had lived a life where I wasn't so naïve.

Lena Ma
The Passion Of My Desolation

Lena Ma
The Passion Of My Desolation

Trapped Inside My Treacherous Body

Lena Ma
The Passion Of My Desolation

I didn't ask for this; I didn't ask to become a her.
You conceived me without my consent, forcing me to become someone I'm not,
Dressing me up in costumes that make living that much harder,
Disciplining me whenever I'm in something different than what you bought.

Tradition tells us to conform to one specific gender,
But society has adapted, norms and rules everchanging.
I choose to be who I feel, and I shall not surrender,
Even if I have to fight with all my years remaining.

Lena Ma
The Passion Of My Desolation

I hear your judgmental words, disappointed at who I've become,
I'm still your child, caged behind the façade you had me entrapped.
I cannot thrive in this body; I will never succumb,
Accept it or not, but between us, you've created a gap.

Equality does not apply only when they adhere to your standards.
Human rights do not exist only when they favor you.
You have given me life, only to fill it with stander,
Like it or not, to you, I will never be true.

Lena Ma
The Passion Of My Desolation

Lena Ma
The Passion Of My Desolation

Lust In My Champagne

Lena Ma
The Passion Of My Desolation

The promises you made had me fallen head over heels,
Giving you my heart, foolishly believing you'll keep it safe.
You took me by the hand and told me what we had was real,
Until you left me in the dust, alone in the streets like a waif.

You promised me the world if I'd just give you my body,
You toasted with a ring and the finest bottle of champagne.
But when those minutes disappeared, you treated me like nobody,
Leaving me for someone else, the love we had in shame.

Lena Ma
The Passion Of My Desolation

I still see the imprint of our love around my finger,
Wishing that someday you'll see the error in your ways.
Ten years later, the thoughts of you still linger,
Still holding onto the memory, counting our days.

I still love you, despite knowing the truth,
That you were only with me to satisfy your lust.
I trusted you, allowing you to take away my youth,
Because of you, in no man will I ever trust.

Lena Ma
The Passion Of My Desolation

Lena Ma
The Passion Of My Desolation

Lena Ma
The Passion Of My Desolation